Teach Me to Knit

Hey kids! Find out how easy it is to make cool stuff for yourself, friends and family, and even your pets. This book shows you everything you need to know to start knitting. You'll have a blast learning the basic steps as you make 13 beginner-level projects that are really awesome! So gather your gear and get ready to knit!

12

36

54

LOOK FOR THE CAMERA in our instructions and watch our technique videos made just for you! www.LeisureArts.com/6648

LEISURE ARTS, INC. • Maumelle, Arkansas

NOTE FOR PARENTS & TEACHERS

When you can link learning with fun, you hold the key to success. Teaching children to knit gives them the creative excitement of making something — plus a real-life way of practicing their math and reading. Developing control of their fine motor skills, such as finger dexterity, is another benefit that will help in many different aspects of their lives.

This book is designed for ages 9 to 14.

Here are a few ways you can heighten a child's enthusiasm for learning to knit:

✳ Encourage youngsters to choose yarn that is eye-catching and huggably soft.

✳ Familiarize yourself with the General Instructions on pages 58-62 in case the child has questions during the lessons.

✳ Make sure the lessons are studied in the order they are presented as each one builds on skills learned in the previous lesson.

✳ Help children notice the tips scattered throughout the lessons. These offer lots of helpful advice that will make learning easier and more fun. Another tip is for you to read the instructions aloud as the child imitates what is seen in the pictures (Figures or Figs.).

✳ Look for the cameras 🎥 in the titles and in the copy accompanied with orange words. These indicate that a video is available online showing the technique or stitch highlighted. The camera will be used the first time the stitch or technique is taught. The techniques will also have a Fig. number and a page number each time they are used so that you can refer back to how they are done. For example, Figs. 16a & b on page 29 shows how to make a knit increase.

Each project will list the items you need for that project in the Shopping List (see the example for the Knit Coaster in the next column). You will also need scissors, a yarn needle, and a tape measure. A crochet hook, size H (5 mm) is used for the occasional dropped stitch.

SHOPPING LIST

Yarn (Medium Weight Cotton)

☐ 20 yards (18.5 meters)
  for **each** Coaster

Knitting Needles

Straight,

☐ Size 8 (5 mm)

Additional Supplies

☐ Safety pin

☐ Yarn needle

Knitting Needles

There are many sizes of knitting needles as shown by the chart below.

KNITTING NEEDLES																			
U.S.	0	1	2	3	4	5	6	7	8	9	10	10½	11	13	15	17	19	35	50
U.K.	13	12	11	10	9	8	7	6	5	4	3	2	1	00	000	---	---	---	---
Metric - mm	2	2.25	2.75	3.25	3.5	3.75	4	4.5	5	5.5	6	6.5	8	9	10	12.75	15	19	25

Knitting needles are numbered. As you can see from the chart, in the US, the higher the number, the larger the needle.

Knitting needles are made straight or circular, with single or double points. The circular needles can be used to knit in a circle or in flat rows just like the straight needles. Double pointed needles are used in sets of four to five needles to knit in smaller circles when the amount of stitches are too few to use a circular needle.

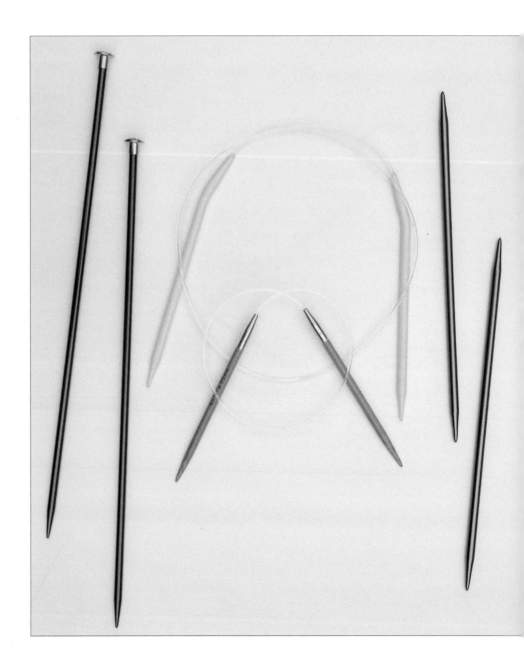

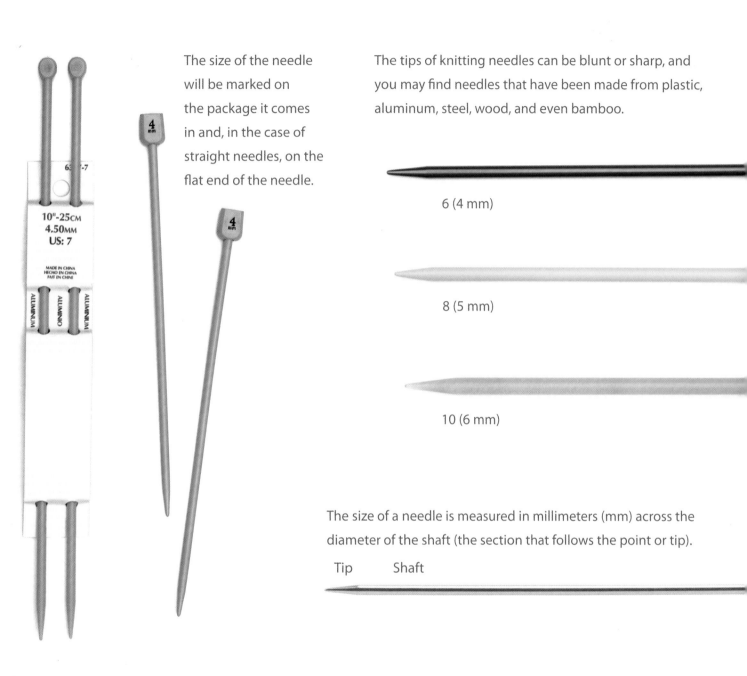

The size of the needle will be marked on the package it comes in and, in the case of straight needles, on the flat end of the needle.

The tips of knitting needles can be blunt or sharp, and you may find needles that have been made from plastic, aluminum, steel, wood, and even bamboo.

6 (4 mm)

8 (5 mm)

10 (6 mm)

The size of a needle is measured in millimeters (mm) across the diameter of the shaft (the section that follows the point or tip).

Tip   Shaft

Knitting Needles you will need:

10" (25.5 cm) straight knitting needles,

✳ a pair of size 8 (5 mm) for learning

✳ a pair of size 10 (6 mm) and

✳ a pair of size 6 (4 mm) for other projects

✳ 24" (61 cm) long circular needle in size 10 (6 mm) for the Ripple Lap Warmer

5

Yarn

Yarn comes in a variety of sizes and colors; you will be using medium weight acrylic or cotton yarn for the projects in this leaflet. When shopping, look on the label for the ball of yarn with the number 4 on it.

Choose any color yarn you like – but not too dark – because lighter colors make it easier to see your stitches.

The label on each skein of yarn will include what the yarn is made of, such as 100% acrylic, 100% wool, 100% cotton, or an acrylic and wool blend.

Variegated yarn is dyed with several different colors and can be fun to use. Many different color combinations are available.

When you remove the label from a new skein of yarn, you'll see a single strand of yarn lying on the outside and tucked into one end of the skein *(see Fig. 1)*. Pull this strand loose. Look at the opposite end of the skein for another strand that comes from the inside – this is the strand that you'll be working with.

Fig. 1

Lace Weight, size 10 crochet thread

Sock, Fingering Baby

Sport, Baby

DK, Light Worsted

Each ball or skein has a paper label that gives information about the yarn such as weight, recommended gauge, color name and number, dye lot number, and washing instructions.

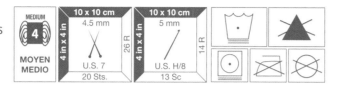

The label can also include the total yards, ounces, grams, and meters in the ball or skein; this makes it easier for you to do the math and figure out how many skeins to buy for the project you want to knit. If you purchase more than one skein of a color, be sure to get the same dye lot number so that the color from one skein to the other will be the same shade.

We recommend that you buy yarn according to the yards listed in the pattern. Ounces and grams can vary from one brand of the same weight to another, but the yards and meters required to knit an item will always remain the same. If you buy yarn according to the ounces or grams listed in a pattern, you may run out of yarn before you finish your project. For instance, if you choose two skeins that are made by two different yarn companies, with each skein weighing 3½ ounces (100 grams), one skein may have 240 yards (219.5 meters) of yarn and the other skein may have 198 yards (181 meters). If the yards or meters are not listed on the label, you may need to buy an extra skein to be sure that you have enough.

Worsted, Afghan, Aran   Chunky, Craft, Rug   Super Bulky, Roving   Jumbo, Roving

Let's start by learning how to make a slip knot to put on your needle.
This is the first step you'll do in all the knit projects you make.

Step 1: Pull enough yarn from the skein to match half the length of your arm. With your right hand, pick up the end of the yarn. Place it behind your left thumb and palm. Hold the yarn end over the working yarn (which is the yarn coming from the skein). Don't let go of the yarn *(see Fig. 2a)*.

Fig. 2a

working yarn

Step 2: With your left hand, take hold of the working yarn *(see Fig. 2b)* and pull it through the loop on your hand to form a new loop *(see Fig. 2c)*. Keep holding that yarn!

Fig. 2b

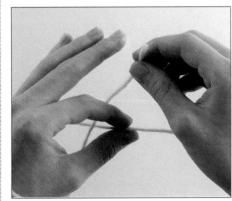

Fig. 2c

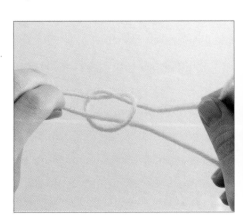

Step 3: Pull the loop until the newly made slip knot is snug but not tight *(see Fig. 2d)*. Now you can let go of the yarn.

Fig. 2d

Step 4: Place the loop on your needle with the working yarn towards your right hand. Pull the working yarn to tighten it around the needle *(see Fig. 2e)*. Keep the loop loose enough to slide easily across the shaft of the needle. The slip knot counts as your first cast on stitch.

Fig. 2e

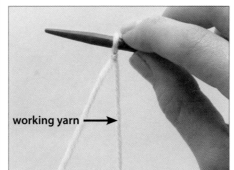

working yarn ⟶

Practice making a slip knot until you're comfortable making one.

To begin knitting, you'll need to cast on a beginning number of stitches onto one needle.

To "un-do" the knot, just slip the needle out of the loop and pull on both ends of the yarn!

DID YOU KNOW?

No one really knows where knitting got started, but some believe it was in Arabia. Just imagine the early nomads toting their knitting gear across the scorching desert sands! Travelers they met along the way picked up on this fascinating and useful skill and took it home with them to Egypt, Spain, and beyond. Among the oldest evidence are scraps of knit fabrics found in ancient Egyptian tombs. WOW!

Lesson 2  Cast On

"Cast on" is a term used to describe placing a beginning number of stitches on the needle.

Step 1: Pull enough yarn from the skein to match the length of your arm. Make a slip knot at that point *(see pages 8 & 9)*, pulling gently on both yarn ends to tighten the stitch on the needle. Remember, this counts as your first cast on stitch.

Step 2: Hold the needle with the stitch on it in your right hand; place the working yarn over your index finger and grip the yarn in your palm with your ring finger and little finger *(see Fig. 3a)*.

Fig. 3a

Step 3: Hold the short end of yarn in the palm of your left hand and loop it from **front** to **back** around your thumb *(see Fig. 3b)*.

Fig. 3b

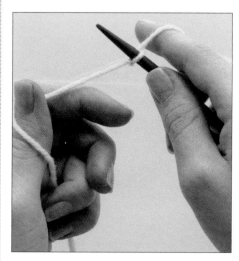

Step 4: Slide the tip of the needle upwards through the yarn loop on your left thumb *(see Fig. 3c)*.

Fig. 3c

Step 5: Take the working yarn over the tip of the needle with your right index finger *(see Fig. 3d)*.

Fig. 3d

Step 6: Pull the yarn and needle down through the loop on your thumb *(see Fig. 3e)*. This forms a stitch.

Fig. 3e

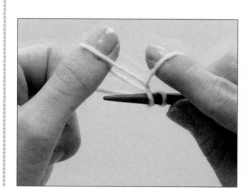

Step 7: Slip your thumb out of the loop. Gently pull the loop to tighten the new stitch on the needle *(see Fig. 3f)*. Catch the end of the yarn to make a new loop on your thumb.

Fig. 3f

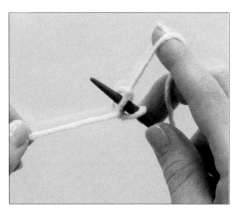

Repeat Steps 4-7 for each new stitch.

To know how much yarn is needed for casting on, allow about 1" (2.5 cm) of yarn for each stitch you cast on. When you work with thinner yarns, it will take slightly less than 1" (2.5 cm) per stitch. Heavier yarns will take a little more than 1" (2.5 cm) per stitch.

Make your cast on stitches snug, but not too tight. The tip of the needle should easily slide into each stitch as you work the first row of knitting.

You may cut the yarn end shorter after you have cast on all your stitches, but make sure you leave an end at least as long as your hand so you can weave it in to hide the end. If the yarn end is going to be used to sew a seam; leave an arm's length, roll it into a ball, and pin it to the bottom of your project until you need it.

Holding the Yarn

Before learning the knit stitch, practice winding the yarn around your right hand. Pass the yarn over the little finger of your right hand, under your two middle fingers, and over your index finger *(see Fig. 4)*. This may feel awkward at first, but controlling the yarn in this way will keep your stitches even.

Fig. 4

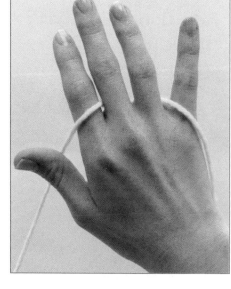

11

The knit stitch is one of two basic stitches of knitting. Knitting every stitch on every row makes a pattern called Garter Stitch, which creates a pebbly, reversible fabric that doesn't curl at the edges.

PROJECT:

●□□□ **BEGINNER**

knit coaster

Now that you know how to cast on (pages 10 & 11), this Coaster will be a breeze to make as you learn how to make the knit stitch. You'll also learn how to finish by binding off your knit stitches.

SHOPPING LIST

Yarn (Medium Weight Cotton)
- ☐ 20 yards (18.5 meters) for **each** Coaster

Knitting Needles

Straight,
- ☐ Size 8 (5 mm)

Additional Supplies

- ☐ Safety pin
- ☐ Yarn needle

Have a pencil and note pad handy to count each row as you knit. You can also buy a row counter to attach to one knitting needle.

Cast on 20 stitches.

ROW 1

Step 1: Hold the needle with the cast on stitches in your left hand and the empty needle in your right hand.

Step 2: With the working yarn in **back** of the needles, insert the tip of the right needle into the stitch closest to the tip of the left needle as shown in **Fig. 5a**.

Fig. 5a

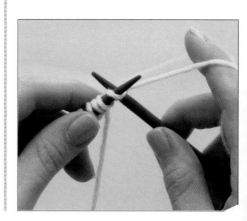

Step 3: Hold the right needle with your left thumb and index finger while you bring the yarn around the right needle and between the needles from **back** to **front** *(see Fig. 5b)*.

Fig. 5b

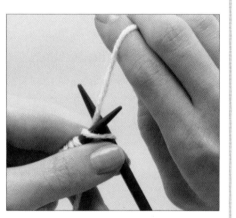

Step 4: With your right hand, bring the tip of the right needle under the left needle, pulling the loop toward you and through the stitch *(see Fig. 5c)*. At the same time, push the old stitch up and off the left needle *(see Fig. 5d)*. Gently pull the working yarn to tighten the new stitch on the shaft of the right needle.

Fig. 5c

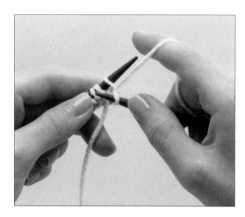

Fig. 5d

Repeat Steps 2-4 across the row.

You have completed one row of 20 stitches. Count the number of stitches after you finish each row to be sure that you haven't accidentally added or dropped a stitch *(see Dropped Stitches, page 60)*.

Attach the safety pin in any stitch on this row. Leave this pin on the Knit Coaster after you have finished it for a surprise in Lesson 4.

ROWS 2-30
To start the next row, switch the needles so the empty needle is in your right hand. The needle with the stitches will be in your left hand.

Repeat Steps 2-4 of Row 1 across the row. You'll still have 20 stitches.

After you complete Row 30, it is time to work the **knit bind off**.

♣ KNIT BIND OFF

Step 1: Knit 2 stitches.

Step 2: Holding the yarn **behind** the work, insert the left needle into the first stitch *(see Fig. 6a)*. Lift the first stitch over the second stitch and off the right needle *(see Fig. 6b)*.

Fig. 6a

Fig. 6b

One stitch has been bound off and one stitch remains on your right needle *(see Fig. 6c)*.

Fig. 6c

Step 3: Knit the next stitch.

Repeat Steps 2 and 3 across the row until only one stitch remains.

It takes two stitches to bind off one stitch. Count each stitch as you bind it off, not as you knit it.

Step 4: To lock the last stitch, cut the working yarn about as long as this page is wide from the needle and bring it up through the last stitch *(see Fig. 6d)*, pulling the yarn to tighten.

Fig. 6d

project ideas:
Make loads of these Coasters in your favorite solid or variegated colors! They also make perfect mats to place under vases, frames, or knickknacks.

WEAVING IN THE YARN ENDS

Step 1: Thread the yarn needle with one of the yarn ends.

Step 2: Weave the yarn loosely through several stitches (*see Fig. 7*). Make sure the yarn is not pulled too tight because that would make your Coaster pucker or wrinkle.

Step 3: Double back and weave the yarn through several stitches in the opposite direction. Clip the end close to the stitches.

Weave in the remaining yarn end.

Fig. 7

PROJECT:

SHOPPING LIST

Yarn (Medium Weight)

☐ 7 yards (6.5 meters)
for **each** Posy

Knitting Needles

Straight,

☐ Size 8 (5 mm)

Additional Supplies

☐ Yarn needle

Have some scrap pieces of yarn or paper clips ready to use as markers. Loop these around the stitches we tell you so that later you'll know which stitches to sew through to form the petals of your Posy.

open petal posy

Practice the cast on (pages 10 & 11) and the knit bind off (page 14) techniques that you've already learned and make the first of what can become a bouquet of pretty Posies.

Cast on 81 stitches.

Step 1: Bind off your first stitch (*see Figs. 6a-c, page 14*) and 📹 place a marker (*see Fig. 8*).

Fig. 8

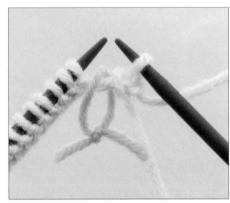

Step 2: Bind off the next 16 stitches and place another marker. Continue binding off 16 stitches and placing markers until there are 15 stitches remaining on the left needle, then bind off the remaining stitches. Leaving an arm's length of yarn for sewing, cut the working yarn.

Thread a yarn needle with the long end. 🎥 Fold the strip like a fan so that all the marked stitches are together *(see Fig. 9a)*. Inserting the needle in the first marked stitch, 🎥 weave the needle and yarn through each marked stitch and through the last bound off stitch *(see Fig. 9b)*. Pull the yarn up tightly. Remove the markers. Knot the yarn ends together, and cut the yarn close to the project.

Fig. 9a

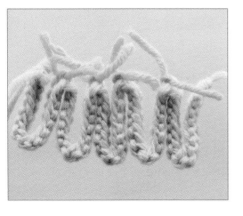

Fig. 9b

project ideas:

Pin, glue, or sew these colorful Posies on hats, bookbags, jackets, purses, shoes, scarves,or photo albums. Stitch or string the Posies together to use as a colorful lampshade trim or glue them to magnets for a special touch on the family fridge. Be sure to make plenty to share with friends!

The purl stitch is the second of the two stitches that form knitting. A purl stitch is the reverse of a knit stitch. When you purl every row, you'll again have a pattern called Garter Stitch like you did when you knit every row!

PROJECT:

 BEGINNER

SHOPPING LIST

Yarn (Medium Weight Cotton)
- ☐ 20 yards (18.5 meters) MEDIUM 4 for **each** Coaster

Knitting Needles

Straight,
- ☐ Size 8 (5 mm)

Additional Supplies
- ☐ Yarn needle

PURL COASTER

As you learn the purl stitch and the purl bind off, you'll be amazed to discover that you've created a reverse twin to your Knit Coaster!

Cast on 20 stitches.

ROW 1

Step 1: Hold the needle with the cast on stitches in your left hand and the empty needle in your right hand.

Step 2: Holding the working yarn in **front** of the needles, insert the tip of the right needle into the front of the stitch closest to the tip of the left needle as shown in **Fig. 10a**.

Fig. 10a

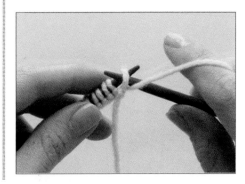

Step 3: Hold the right needle with your left thumb and index finger while you bring the yarn **between** the needles from **right** to **left** and around the right needle *(see Fig. 10b)*.

Fig. 10b

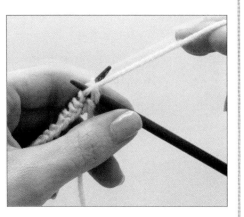

Step 4: With your right hand, move the tip of the right needle under the left needle through the stitch, pulling the loop away from you *(see Fig. 10c)*. At the same time, push the old stitch up and off the left needle *(see Fig. 10d)*. Gently pull the working yarn to tighten the new stitch on the shaft of the right needle.

Fig. 10c

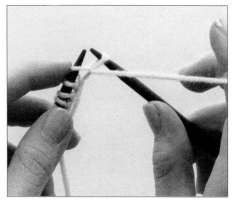

Fig. 10d

Repeat Steps 2-4 across the row.

You've completed one row of 20 stitches.

ROWS 2-30

To start the next row, switch the needles so the empty needle is in your right hand. The needle with the stitches will be in your left hand.

Repeat Steps 2-4 of Row 1 across the row. You'll still have 20 stitches.

After you complete Row 30, it's time to work the **purl bind off**.

🎥 PURL BIND OFF

Step 1: Purl 2 stitches.

Step 2: Holding the yarn in front of the work, insert the left needle into the first stitch *(see Fig. 11a)*. Lift the first stitch over the second stitch and off the right needle *(see Fig. 11b)*.

Fig. 11a

Fig. 11b

One stitch has been bound off and one stitch remains on your right needle *(see Fig. 11c)*.

Fig. 11c

Step 3: Purl the next stitch.

Repeat Steps 2 and 3 across the row until only one stitch remains.

Cut the working yarn about as long as this page is wide from the needle and bring it up through the last stitch *(see Fig. 6d, page 14)*, pulling the yarn end to tighten.

Weave in the yarn ends *(see Fig. 7, page 15)*.

Compare your new Purl Coaster to your Knit Coaster. Surprise! If you didn't have the safety pin still on the Knit Coaster, you'd have a hard time telling them apart!

DiD you Know?

During World Wars I and II, school-age children joined community efforts to knit scarves, sweaters, and socks for the soldiers. Modern knitters are known for their big hearts and generosity, using their knitting to make warm caps, wraps, and clothing for the less fortunate. No matter where you live, you're sure to find groups making items to donate to children's hospitals, charities, and world relief organizations. What a great reason to learn to knit!

LESSON 5 🎥 Basic Fabrics

Using the two stitches you've just learned — knit and purl — you can easily make the following fabrics.

You've already learned how to make 🎥 Garter Stitch fabric by knitting or purling every stitch on every row (see Knit Coaster, page 12, or Purl Coaster, page 18).

If you knit one row and then purl the next row, you'll be making 🎥 Stockinette Stitch, which is the most common knit fabric.

If you alternate knit and purl stitches across the first row, then knit into the purl stitches and purl into the knit stitches as they face you on the next row, you'll be making 🎥 Seed Stitch. Seed Stitch is a reversible fabric that does not curl at the edges and is also known as Moss Stitch.

Garter Stitch

Stockinette Stitch

Seed Stitch

Ribbing is a stretchy fabric that is often worked at the bottom of sweaters, on cuffs, and around necklines. You alternate the knit and purl stitches on the first row. On the following rows, you'll knit the knit stitches and purl the purl stitches as they face you. The most common ribbings are 🎥 knit 1, purl 1 and 🎥 knit 2, purl 2.

Knit 1, Purl 1 Ribbing

Knit 2, Purl 2 Ribbing

You can knit a washcloth in cotton yarn while you practice Garter Stitch and learn Stockinette Stitch and Seed Stitch. Then you can knit a Soft Drink Cozy to learn how to knit Ribbing and to work "decreases."

COTTON WASHCLOTH

You know how to knit (page 12) and how to purl (page 18), so let's combine the two stitches now while knitting this washcloth to create a different look!

PROJECT:

 BEGINNER

SHOPPING LIST

Yarn (Medium Weight Cotton)

☐ 45 yards (41 meters) MEDIUM 4

Knitting Needles

Straight,

☐ Size 8 (5 mm)

Additional Supplies

☐ Yarn needle

Cast on 31 stitches.

Rows 1-10: Knit each stitch across the row (**Garter Stitch made**): you'll have 31 stitches.

Row 11: Purl each stitch across the row: you'll still have 31 stitches and should continue to have 31 stitches through Row 47.

Row 12: Knit each stitch across the row.

Row 13: Purl each stitch across the row.

Rows 14 and 15: Repeat Rows 12 and 13 (**Stockinette Stitch made**).

When you see a ★ (star) in the instructions, it means that you should work the instructions following the first ★ once, then repeat only those instructions as many times as we say **plus** the first time. We will either say how many times, as in "repeat from ★ 2 times **more**," or you will find an instruction such as "repeat from ★ across" or "repeat from ★ across to the last 4 stitches." In the last case, you would work the instructions repeated from the ★ across the row until you have 4 stitches left, then you would be told what to do with the last 4 stitches.

Rows 16-21: Knit the first stitch, ★ bring the working yarn **between** the needles to the **front** and purl the next stitch, bring the working yarn **between** the needles to the **back** and knit the next stitch; repeat from ★ across the row (**Seed Stitch made**).

PROJECT IDEAS:

Make one washcloth for the tub and one for the sink or how about letting one become a dishcloth? Yuck, who wants to think about dishes, right? But you'll be amazed how great your washcloth cleans those yucky dishes!

Rows 22-27: Repeat Rows 12 and 13, 3 times (**Stockinette Stitch made**).

Rows 28-33: Repeat Rows 16-21 (**Seed Stitch made**).

Rows 34-38: Repeat Rows 12 and 13 twice; then repeat Row 12 once **more** (**Stockinette Stitch made**).

Rows 39-47: Knit each stitch across the row (**Garter Stitch made**).

Bind off all stitches in **knit**.

Weave in the yarn ends.

PROJECT:

■□□□ BEGINNER

SOFT DRINK COZY

The most common ribbing pattern is knit 1, purl 1 ribbing. You'll make a Soft Drink Cozy while you practice ribbing (see Basic Fabrics, page 21). You'll also learn how to decrease to shape the bottom of the Cozy. A decrease is made when two or more stitches are worked together to form one stitch.

SHOPPING LIST

Yarn (Medium Weight Cotton)
☐ 30 yards (27.5 meters) **MEDIUM 4**

Knitting Needles
Straight,
☐ Size 8 (5 mm)

Additional Supplies
☐ Yarn needle

Cast on 36 stitches.

Row 1 (Right side): ★ Knit 1, purl 1; repeat from ★ across the row: you will have 18 knit stitches and 18 purl stitches.

Note: Loop a short piece of yarn around any stitch to mark Row 1 as **right** side.

Rows 2-20: ★ Knit 1, purl 1; repeat from ★ across the row: you will have 18 knit stitches and 18 purl stitches.

ROW 21
Step 1: Knit 4.

Now, you are ready to work the knit 2 stitches together decrease.

Step 2: Insert the right needle into the **front** of the first two stitches on the left needle as if to **knit** *(see Fig. 12a).*

Fig. 12a

Step 3: Knit the two stitches together as if they were one stitch *(see Fig. 12b)*. (The knit 2 together decrease slants to the **right** on the knit side.)

Fig. 12b

Note: Each decrease subtracts one stitch from the amount of stitches on your needle.

Step 4: ★ Knit 4, then knit the next two stitches together; repeat from ★ across the row: you'll now have 30 stitches.

HERE'S THE LATEST SPIN:

Today everyone — rich or poor — can enjoy comfortable knit clothing. That's because the girls who spun the yarn refused to let the royal knitting guilds prevent them from learning to knit and making clothes for their own families.

ROW 22

Step 1: Purl 5.

Now, you are ready to work the purl two stitches together decrease.

Step 2: Keep the working yarn in front of the needles while you insert the right needle into the **front** of the first two stitches on the left needle as if to **purl** *(see Fig. 13a)*.

Fig. 13a

Step 3: Purl the two stitches together as if they were one stitch *(see Fig. 13b)*. (The purl 2 together decrease slants to the **right** on the knit side.)

Fig. 13b

Note: Each decrease subtracts one stitch from the amount of stitches on your needle.

Step 4: Purl 3, ★ purl the next 2 stitches together, purl 3; repeat from ★ across the row: you'll now have 25 stitches.

Row 23: Knit 1, ★ knit the next 2 stitches together, knit 4; repeat from ★ across the row: you'll now have 21 stitches.

Row 24: Purl 3, ★ purl the next 2 stitches together, purl 1; repeat from ★ across the row: you'll now have 15 stitches.

Row 25: ★ Knit 1, knit the next 2 stitches together; repeat from ★ across the row: you'll now have 10 stitches.

When you have instructions inside parentheses ( ), repeat only those instructions in the parentheses as many times as we say on the outside of the parentheses.

Row 26: (Purl the next 2 stitches together) 5 times: you'll now have 5 stitches.

Leaving the 5 stitches on the needle, cut the working yarn an arm's length from the needle.

Thread a yarn needle with the length of yarn and  weave it through the stitches on the needle *(see Fig. 14)*, removing the knitting needle and pulling the stitches closed tightly. Do not cut the yarn or remove the yarn needle.

Fig. 14

With the **right** side of the Cozy folded to the inside and lining up the rows, whipstitch the seam as follows: ★ insert the needle from **back** to **front** through both edges and pull the yarn through *(see Fig. 15)*; repeat from ★ across.

Fig. 15

Weave in the yarn ends.

Turn Cozy right side out.

project ideas:

For a special touch, make a Cozy to match your Coasters. The Cozy will keep your hand warm while you drink a cold can of your favorite 12-ounce beverage.

picture this

Did you know that some famous Hollywood stars knit on their movie sets, to pass the time during filming breaks or help them relax? Someday you may chase your dreams into tinsel town, so why not get a head-start and learn to knit before your big debut? And the winner is … you!

In this lesson, you'll practice the knit two together decrease (pages 24 & 25) and learn how to increase stitches as you make a stuffed toy ball for your dog. You'll also practice Stockinette Stitch (page 21) and learn to weave a seam closed.

PROJECT:

 BEGINNER

SHOPPING LIST

Yarn (Medium Weight) **4**

☐ Small - 24 yards (22 meters)

☐ Medium - 32 yards
(29.5 meters) **each** of 2 colors
(We used 2 strands of the
same color.)

☐ Large - 36 yards (33 meters)
each of 3 colors

Knitting Needles

Straight,

☐ Size 8 (5 mm) for Small Ball

☐ Size 10 (6 mm) for Medium **and**
Large Balls

Additional Supplies

☐ Yarn needle

☐ Scrap yarn or polyester fiberfill
for stuffing

DOG'S TOY BALL

You can make this toy using one strand of medium weight yarn and the size 8 needles you began your lessons with. Follow the same basic ball pattern to make larger toys in more than one color. With the larger projects, you'll learn to knit with multiple strands of yarn held together while using a size 10 needle. Make one of each size and compare them when you're finished.

BASIC BALL

Follow the instructions using one strand of yarn and the smaller size needles to make the Small Ball. After you're comfortable with the pattern and with working the increases and decreases, you can make the Medium Ball by holding two strands of yarn together and using the larger size needles. Treat the two strands of yarn as if you were knitting with one strand of yarn. The Large Ball is knit by holding three strands of yarn together and using the larger size needles.

Cast on 6 stitches (be sure you cast on **loosely** so you can work the 🎥 knit increase easily in each stitch on Row 1).

ROW 1

Step 1: Knit the first stitch but do **not** slip it off the left needle *(see Fig. 16a)*.

Fig. 16a

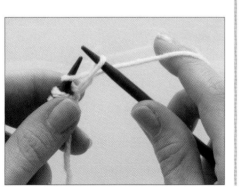

Step 2: Instead, knit into the **back** of the **same** stitch *(see Fig. 16b)*, then slip it off the left needle. You now have two stitches on the right needle and have made your first knit increase.

Fig. 16b

Step 3: Repeat Steps 1 and 2 to increase in each remaining stitch across the row: you'll now have 12 stitches.

Row 2: Purl each stitch across the row: you'll still have 12 stitches.

Row 3: Increase in each stitch across the row: you'll now have 24 stitches.

Row 4: Purl each stitch across the row: you'll still have 24 stitches.

Row 5: Increase in each stitch across the row: you'll now have 48 stitches.

Row 6: Purl each stitch across the row: you'll still have 48 stitches and should continue to have 48 stitches through Row 20.

Row 7: Knit each stitch across the row.

Row 8: Purl each stitch across the row.

Rows 9-20: Repeat Rows 7 and 8, 6 times.

Sometimes a set of parentheses will be followed by a direction, such as "across" or "across to the last 4 stitches," instead of a number. In these cases, you'll repeat the instructions inside the parentheses until you've finished the row or reached the number of stitches we say. Then, you'd be told how to work the remaining stitches.

Row 21: (Knit 2 stitches together) across the row *(see Figs. 12a & b, pages 24 & 25)*: you'll now have 24 stitches.

Row 22: Purl each stitch across the row: you'll still have 24 stitches.

Row 23: (Knit 2 stitches together) across the row: you'll now have 12 stitches.

Row 24: Purl each stitch across the row: you'll still have 12 stitches.

Row 25: (Knit 2 stitches together) across the row; cut the working yarn leaving a long end for sewing: you'll now have 6 stitches.

Thread a yarn needle with the long end and weave it through the 6 stitches on the needle *(see Fig. 14, page 27)*, removing the knitting needle and pulling the stitches closed tightly. Make a knot to secure the yarn. Do not remove the yarn needle and do not cut the yarn end.

Make the yarn stuffing: Using leftover yarn, wrap the yarn 18 times around 4 fingers of one hand twice. This is about 6 yards (5.5 meters) of yarn. Cut and set aside. Repeat this as many times as needed.

Weave the seam: With the **right** side of the piece facing you and the edges lined up, insert the needle under the bar between the first and second stitches on the row and pull the yarn through *(see Fig. 17)*.

Fig. 17

Insert the needle under the next bar on the second side. Repeat from side to side across **only** half of the seam, being careful to line up the rows and pulling the seam closed as you work.

Stuff the toy firmly with scrap yarn or polyester fiberfill.

Finish weaving the seam, stuffing the toy as you go. Weave the yarn end through the beginning 6 stitches; pull the yarn tightly to close and make a knot to secure the yarn. Insert the needle inside the ball and push it out the other side. Cut the yarn end close to the ball.

Shape the Ball with your hands like you are making a snowball.

project ideas:

Play with color combos and types of yarn to make balls with different patterns. When you are comfortable with this pattern and are creating these toys in no time, you may want to consider donating a few to a local veterinary clinic or animal rescue service.

LESSON 7 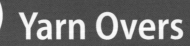 Yarn Overs

You can create a new stitch by simply looping your yarn around your needle. This loop is an increase called a yarn over. A yarn over produces a hole in the fabric and is usually paired with a decrease to create a lacy look or a buttonhole for a sweater or vest. Yarn overs are made in different ways depending on the type of stitch worked before and after the yarn over (pages 61 & 62).

scarf

As you knit this warm Scarf, you'll learn how to make one kind of yarn over. This yarn over has knit stitches before and after it. You'll also be using the knit two together decrease (pages 24 & 25). Since you're pairing each yarn over with a decrease, you'll see that your amount of stitches will remain the same.

BEGINNER

SHOPPING LIST

Yarn (Medium Weight) **4**
[6 ounces, 315 yards
(170 grams, 288 meters) per skein]:
☐ 1 skein

Knitting Needles

Straight,
☐ Size 8 (5 mm)

Additional Supplies

☐ Yarn needle

Cast on 33 stitches.

Rows 1-3: Knit each stitch across the row: you'll have 33 stitches.

ROW 4
Step 1: Knit 3.

You are ready to make your first yarn over. The yarn over in Step 2 will replace the stitch that the knit two stitches together decrease in Step 3 will take away so your number of stitches will stay the same.

Step 2: Bring the yarn forward **between** the needles and then back **over** the top of the right needle so that it's in position to knit the next stitch (see Fig. 18). You've just made your first yarn over.

Fig. 18

Step 3: Knit 2 stitches together *(see Figs. 12a & b, pages 24 & 25)*, knit 3, ★ yarn over, knit 2 stitches together, knit 3; repeat from ★ across: you'll still have 33 stitches.

On the row following a yarn over, be careful to keep the yarn over on the needle and treat it like a stitch by knitting or purling it as instructed.

ROW 5

Step 1: Knit 4.

Step 2: Knit the yarn over in the same way as you'd knit a stitch *(see Figs. 19a & b).*

Fig. 19a

Fig. 19b

Step 3: Knit each stitch across the rest of the row: you should still have 33 stitches and should continue to have 33 stitches through the entire Scarf.

Rows 6 and 7: Knit each stitch across the row.

Row 8: Knit 5, yarn over, knit 2 stitches together, ★ knit 3, yarn over, knit 2 stitches together; repeat from ★ across to the last 6 stitches, knit 6.

Rows 9-11: Knit each stitch across the row.

DID YOU KNOW?

If you'd lived in 16th century Europe, you might have grown up to be a master knitter making the beautiful clothes worn only by kings, princes, and other members of nobility. That would have been like having your own designer line, with your name on the label — all because you learned to knit!

Row 12: Knit 3, ★ yarn over, knit 2 stitches together, knit 3; repeat from ★ across.

Rows 13-15: Knit each stitch across the row.

Repeat Rows 8-15 until your Scarf is about 45" (114 cm) long.

Bind off all stitches in **knit** *(see Figs. 6a-c, page 14)*.

Weave in the yarn ends.

PROJECT IDEAS:

Imagine the amazement of your friends when you show up at the ballgame wearing a scarf in the school colors! Or you can make extra scarves to help out community services that collect warm clothing for needy children each winter.

To "slip" a stitch, you move it from one needle to the other without working into it. Slipped stitches are used in shaping decreases or in stitch patterns.

PROJECT:

Ripple Lap Wrap

To make this lap-sized Wrap, you need to know the knit two together decrease (pages 24 & 25) and how to yarn over (page 32). You'll learn another decrease that has a slipped stitch passed over a knit stitch and will find out about "gauge."

 BEGINNER

Finished Size: 31" wide by 43" long (78.5 cm by 109 cm)

SHOPPING LIST

Yarn (Medium Weight) 4

[6 ounces, 315 yards
(170 grams, 288 meters) per skein]:

☐ Purple - 1 skein

☐ Pink - 1 skein

☐ Blue - 1 skein

☐ Green - 1 skein

☐ Yellow - 1 skein

[4 ounces, 204 yards
(113 grams, 186 meters) per skein]:

☐ Variegated - 1 skein

Knitting Needle

24" (61 cm) Circular

☐ Size 10 (6 mm)

or size needed for gauge

(see Gauge, page 59)

Additional Supplies

☐ Yarn needle

For this Wrap to be the right size and not be so big that it would fit your bed or so small that it would be doll-sized, you must get "gauge." Your gauge is the number of stitches and rows you have for every inch of knitting. Make the Gauge Swatch below; if it's larger than a 3" (7.5 cm) square, use a smaller size of needles. If the swatch is smaller than a 3" (7.5 cm) square, use a larger size of needles.

Always make a gauge swatch before beginning your project.

GAUGE INFORMATION

In Stockinette Stitch *(see page 21)*,

12 stitches and 15 rows = 3" (7.5 cm)

Gauge Swatch: 3" (7.5 cm) square

Cast on 12 stitches.

Row 1: Purl each stitch across the row.

Row 2: Knit each stitch across the row.

Rows 3-15: Repeat Rows 1 and 2, 6 times; then repeat Row 1 once **more**.

Bind off all stitches in **knit**.

A circular needle can be used just like straight needles, turning your work after every row. If you have a lot of stitches in a project, a circular needle can be easier to use than straight needles.

With Purple, cast on 137 stitches.

Rows 1-5: Knit each stitch across the row.

You will learn how to  change colors at the end of Row 5.

Step 1: Cut Purple, making sure to leave a 6" (15 cm) length of yarn to weave in later.

Step 2: Loosely tie Pink onto the Purple with a single knot *(see Fig. 20)*, leaving a 6" (15 cm) length of Pink to weave in later. Make sure your knot is not too tight because you'll want to untie it when you begin weaving in the yarn ends.

Fig. 20

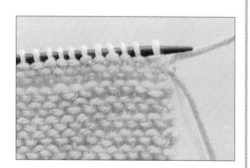

The next decrease is called  slip 1 as if to **knit**, knit 1, pass the slipped stitch over the knit stitch.

Row 6: With Pink, knit 2, ★ knit 2 stitches together *(see Figs. 12a & b, pages 24 & 25)*, knit 7, yarn over *(see Fig. 18, page 32)*, knit 1, yarn over, knit 7, slip 1 stitch as if to **knit** *(see Fig. 21a)*, knit 1, pass the slipped stitch over the knit stitch *(see Fig. 21b)* and off the right needle; repeat from ★ across to the last 2 stitches, knit 2: you'll still have 137 stitches.

Fig. 21a   **Fig. 21b**

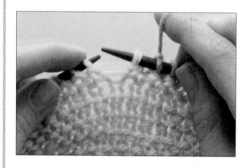   

Row 7: Knit 2, purl each stitch across to the last 2 stitches, knit 2: you'll still have 137 stitches and should continue to have 137 stitches through the entire Wrap.

Row 8: Knit 2, ★ knit 2 stitches together, knit 7, yarn over, knit 1, yarn over, knit 7, slip 1 stitch as if to **knit**, knit 1, pass the slipped stitch over the knit stitch; repeat from ★ across to the last 2 stitches, knit 2.

Row 9: Knit 2, purl each stitch across to the last 2 stitches, knit 2, cut Pink.

Row 10: With Blue, knit 2, ★ knit 2 stitches together, knit 7, yarn over, knit 1, yarn over, knit 7, slip 1 stitch as if to **knit**, knit 1, pass the slipped stitch over the knit stitch; repeat from ★ across to the last 2 stitches, knit 2.

Row 11: Knit 2, purl each stitch across to the last 2 stitches, knit 2.

Rows 12 and 13: Repeat Rows 10 and 11; at the end of Row 13, cut Blue.

Rows 14-17: With Green, repeat Rows 10 and 11 twice; at the end of Row 17, cut Green.

Rows 18-21: With Yellow, repeat Rows 10 and 11 twice; at the end of Row 21, cut Yellow.

Rows 22-25: With Variegated, repeat Rows 10 and 11 twice; at the end of Row 25, cut Variegated.

Rows 26-29: With Purple, repeat Rows 10 and 11 twice; at the end of Row 29, cut Purple.

Rows 30-33: With Pink, repeat Rows 10 and 11 twice; at the end of Row 33, cut Pink.

Rows 34-209: Repeat Rows 10-33, 7 times; then repeat Rows 10-17 once **more.**

Rows 210-214: With Purple, knit each stitch across the row.

Bind off all stitches in **knit.**

Weave in the yarn ends.

project ideas:

You can make the Lap Wrap all in one color but it's really fun to mix up lots of colors! Make extra Lap Wraps to donate to the children's ward in a local hospital or to a nursing home.

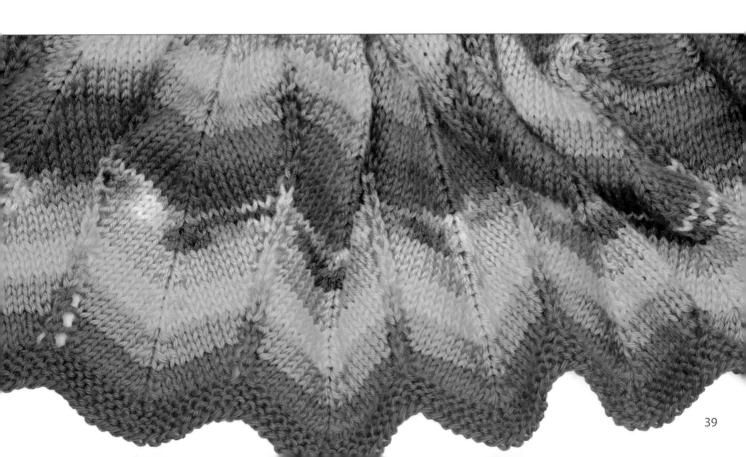

You have increased stitches by knitting into the front and the back of a stitch (page 29). If you look at the Ball, you can see a little "bar" where the stitch was increased. A Make One increase is much harder to spot and doesn't use any stitches from the left needle.

PROJECT:

■□□□□ **BEGINNER**

PILLOW

Work wedges in Stockinette Stitch (page 21) by increasing stitches using a method called Make One. Sew all the wedges together to make a colorful addition to your bedroom or any room in your home!

Finished Size: 16" (40.5 cm) diameter

SHOPPING LIST

Yarn (Medium Weight)
[6 ounces, 315 yards
(170 grams, 288 meters) per skein]:

☐ Blue - 1 skein

☐ Yellow - 1 skein

☐ Purple - 1 skein

☐ Green - 1 skein

Knitting Needle

Straight,

☐ Size 8 (5 mm)

or size needed for gauge

(see Gauge, page 59)

Additional Supplies

☐ Polyester fiberfill

☐ Fabric for pillow form

☐ Yarn needle

GAUGE INFORMATION

In Stockinette Stitch *(see page 21)*,
   18 stitches and 24 rows = 4" (10 cm)

Gauge Swatch: 4" (10 cm) square
Cast on 18 stitches.

Row 1: Knit each stitch across the row.

Row 2: Purl each stitch across the row.

Rows 3-24: Repeat Rows 1 and 2, 11 times.

Bind off all stitches in **knit**.

PILLOW WEDGE

Make 4 Wedges **each** in the following colors for a total of 16 Wedges - Blue, Yellow, Purple, and Green.

Place a slip knot on the needle: one stitch.

Row 1: Increase by knitting in the front and the back of the stitch *(see Figs. 16a & b, page 29)*: you'll have 2 stitches.

Now, you are ready to learn the  Make One increase.

Row 2: Purl 2.

ROW 3

Step 1: Knit the first stitch.

Step 2: Insert your left needle from **front** to **back** under the strand of yarn **between** the stitch you just worked and the next stitch *(see Fig. 22a)*.

Fig. 22a

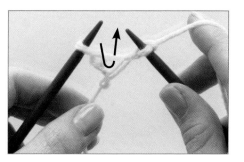

Step 3: Knit into the back of this strand *(see Fig. 22b)*. You have completed a Make One increase.

Fig. 22b

Step 4: Knit the last stitch: you'll now have 3 stitches and should continue to have 3 stitches through Row 6.

Row 4: Purl each stitch across the row.

Row 5: Knit each stitch across the row.

Row 6: Purl each stitch across the row.

Row 7: Knit 1, Make One, knit each stitch across to the last stitch, Make One, knit the last stitch: you'll now have 5 stitches.

Row 8: Purl each stitch across the row.

Row 9: Knit 1, Make One, knit each stitch across to the last stitch, Make One, knit the last stitch: you'll now have 7 stitches.

Rows 10-33: Repeat Rows 4-9, 4 times: you'll now have 23 stitches.

Rows 34-45: Repeat Rows 4-7, 3 times: you'll now have 29 stitches.

Row 46: Purl each stitch across the row: you'll still have 29 stitches.

Bind off all stitches in **knit**, leaving a long end for sewing.

FINISHING

Weave 8 Wedges together *(see Fig. 17, page 30)* forming the Front of the Pillow; then weave the remaining 8 Wedges together to form the Back.

Make a pillow form: Using the Front as a pattern, cut two pieces of fabric adding ¼" (7.5 mm) for the seam allowance around the entire edge. With **right** sides together, sew the seam, leaving a 2" (5 cm) opening for turning. Turn the form right side out. Stuff the pillow form with polyester fiberfill; then sew the opening closed.

With **wrong** sides together, whipstitch the back and the front of the Pillow together *(see Fig. 15, page 27)*, putting the pillow form inside before finishing the seam.

PROJECT IDEAS:

You may choose to sew large buttons to the center front and back of your Pillow or attach a Posy (page 16) to each side for a designer touch. Another idea would be to change colors on the same row on each wedge to create a circular stripe! Or how about color coordinating the wedges of your Pillow to match the Lap Wrap (page 43) for a decorator touch?

MORE FUN PROJECTS

Here are four additional projects selected especially for the beginning knitter. While you've learned a lot of what you need to know to make these projects, we'll teach you some new techniques and refer you back to previous lessons as a way of reinforcing your new skills, too!

cat's toy fish

Practice increasing by knitting in the front and back of a stitch (page 29) and decreasing by knitting two stitches together (pages 24 & 25), plus learn the knit three stitches together decrease to make a fish-shapedtoy to entertain your kitty!

 **BEGINNER**

SHOPPING LIST

Yarn (Medium Weight)

- ☐ 13 yards (12 meters) for **each** Fish
- ☐ 18" (45.5 cm) length for eyes
- ☐ Scrap yarn for stuffing

Knitting Needles

Straight,

- ☐ Size 8 (5 mm)

Additional Supplies

- ☐ 36" (91.5 cm) straight stick for fishing pole
- ☐ Clear fishing line - 36" (91.5 cm) length
- ☐ Yarn needle

FISH

SIDE (Make 2)

Cast on 9 stitches.

Row 1: Purl each stitch across the row: you'll have 9 stitches.

Row 2: Knit 2 stitches together *(see Figs. 12a & b, pages 24 & 25)*, knit 5, knit 2 stitches together: you'll now have 7 stitches.

Row 3: Purl each stitch across the row: you'll still have 7 stitches.

Row 4: Knit 2 stitches together, knit 3, knit 2 stitches together: you'll now have 5 stitches.

Row 5: Purl each stitch across the row: you'll still have 5 stitches.

Row 6: Knit 2 stitches together, knit 1, knit 2 stitches together: you'll now have 3 stitches.

Row 7: Purl each stitch across the row: you'll still have 3 stitches.

Row 8: Increase in the first stitch *(see Figs. 16a & b, page 29)*, knit 1, increase in the last stitch: you'll now have 5 stitches.

Row 9: Purl each stitch across the row: you'll still have 5 stitches.

Row 10: Increase in the first stitch, knit 3, increase in the last stitch: you'll now have 7 stitches.

Row 11: Purl each stitch across the row: you'll still have 7 stitches.

Row 12: Increase in the first stitch, knit 5, increase in the last stitch: you'll now have 9 stitches.

Row 13: Purl each stitch across the row: you'll still have 9 stitches.

Row 14: Increase in the first stitch, knit 7, increase in the last stitch: you'll now have 11 stitches.

Row 15: Purl each stitch across the row: you'll still have 11 stitches.

Row 16: Increase in the first stitch, knit 9, increase in the last stitch: you'll now have 13 stitches.

Row 17: Purl each stitch across the row: you'll still have 13 stitches.

Row 18: Knit 2 stitches together, knit 9, knit 2 stitches together: you'll now have 11 stitches.

Row 19: Purl each stitch across the row: you'll still have 11 stitches.

Row 20: Knit 2 stitches together, knit 7, knit 2 stitches together: you'll now have 9 stitches.

Row 21: Purl each stitch across the row: you'll still have 9 stitches.

Row 22: Knit 2 stitches together, knit 5, knit 2 stitches together: you'll now have 7 stitches.

Row 23: Purl each stitch across the row: you'll still have 7 stitches.

Row 24: Knit 2 stitches together, knit 3, knit 2 stitches together: you'll now have 5 stitches.

Row 25: Purl each stitch across the row: you'll still have 5 stitches.

Row 26: Knit 2 stitches together, knit 1, knit 2 stitches together: you'll now have 3 stitches.

Row 27: Purl each stitch across the row: you'll still have 3 stitches.

Now, you are ready to learn the ▶️ knit 3 stitches together decrease.

Row 28: Insert the right needle into the **front** of the three stitches on the left needle as if to **knit** *(see Fig. 23)*, then knit them together as if they were one stitch: you'll now have one stitch.

Fig. 23

Cut the working yarn leaving a long end for sewing; pull the end through the stitch on the needle and tighten.

FINISHING

Make the yarn stuffing: Using leftover yarn, wrap the yarn 18 times around 4 fingers of one hand. This is about 3 yards (2.5 meters) of yarn. Cut and set aside.

▶️ **Sew the seam:** Thread the yarn needle with either long end. Holding the **right** sides of the pieces together, line up the rows along the side edges and sew across one edge *(see Fig. 24)*. Knot the end to secure; do not cut the end.

Fig. 24

Thread the yarn needle with the second yarn end and sew the remaining side seam. Turn the piece right side out, placing the first yarn end inside the body. Add the yarn stuffing inside the body of the Fish (do not stuff the tail); sew the tail shut. Knot the end to secure, then insert the yarn needle inside the Fish and push it out the other side. Cut the yarn end close to the Fish.

▶️ **Make the eyes:** Cut two 9" (23 cm) lengths of contrasting color yarn. Thread the yarn needle with one length of yarn.

Insert the needle through a stitch on each side of the head, leaving an end hanging loose on each side *(see Fig. 25a)*. Remove the yarn needle.

Fig. 25a

Thread the yarn needle with the second length of yarn. Move over one stitch from where the first length of yarn is and insert the needle through the head, leaving an end hanging loose on each side. Remove the yarn needle.

On one side of the head, tie a knot, being careful not to pull the other ends out of the opposite side (*see Fig. 25b*).

Fig. 25b

Tie a knot on the other side of the head. Cut the yarn close to each knot and fluff the ends (*see Fig. 25c*).

Fig. 25c

Put it all together: Tie the clear fishing line securely to the end of the pole. (An adult can cut a small slit in the end of the pole to keep the line from slipping off).

Tie the loose end of the fishing line to the top of the Fish in the center of the back (*see Fig. 26*).

Fig. 26

project idea:

Add a little catnip to the stuffing as an extra treat for your kitty! Or hang a school of Fish at different levels in a doorway to create a cat activity.

Leg warmers

Ribbing (page 21) and the knit two together decrease
(pages 24 & 25) shape these Leg Warmers for active girls!

◖☐☐☐▷ **BEGINNER**

Finished Size: 26¾" (68 cm) long

SHOPPING LIST

Yarn (Medium Weight)

[6 ounces, 315 yards
(170 grams, 288 meters) per skein]:

☐ 1 skein

Knitting Needles

Straight,

☐ Size 6 (4 mm) **and**

☐ Size 8 (5 mm)

   or sizes needed for gauge
   (see Gauge, page 59)

Additional Supplies

☐ Yarn needle

GAUGE INFORMATION

With larger size needles,

   in Stockinette Stitch *(see page 21)*,

   18 stitches and 24 rows = 4" (10 cm)

Gauge Swatch: 4" (10 cm) square
With larger size needles, cast on
18 stitches.

Row 1 (Right side)**:** Knit each stitch
across the row.

Row 2: Purl each stitch across the
row.

Rows 3-24: Repeat Rows 1 and 2,
11 times.

Bind off all stitches in **knit**.

LEG WARMER (Make 2)
UPPER CUFF

With larger size needles, cast on
44 stitches **loosely**.

Row 1: (Knit 1, purl 1) across: you'll
have 22 knit stitches and 22 purl
stitches.

Repeat Row 1 until Upper Cuff
measures 4" (10 cm).

BODY

Work in Stockinette Stitch (knit one
row, purl one row) until the piece
measures about 21" (53.5 cm) from
the cast on edge, ending by working
a **purl** row.

SHAPING

Row 1: Knit 1, knit 2 stitches together *(see Figs. 12a & b, pages 24 & 25)*, knit each stitch across to the last 3 stitches, knit 2 stitches together, knit 1: you'll now have 42 stitches and should continue to have 42 stitches through Row 4.

Row 2: Purl each stitch across the row.

Row 3: Knit each stitch across the row.

Row 4: Purl each stitch across the row.

Row 5: Knit 1, knit 2 stitches together, knit each stitch across to the last 3 stitches, knit 2 stitches together, knit 1: you'll now have 40 stitches and should continue to have 40 stitches through Row 8.

Rows 6-8: Repeat Rows 2-4.

Row 9: Knit 1, knit 2 stitches together, knit each stitch across to the last 3 stitches, knit 2 stitches together, knit 1: you'll now have 38 stitches and should continue to have 38 stitches through Row 12.

Rows 10-12: Repeat Rows 2-4.

Row 13: Knit 1, knit 2 stitches together, knit each stitch across to the last 3 stitches, knit 2 stitches together, knit 1: you'll have 36 stitches and should continue to have 36 stitches through Row 16.

Rows 14-16: Repeat Rows 2-4.

LOWER CUFF

Begin using the smaller size needles.

Changing needle sizes is easy! Just work one row using one of the new size needles in your right hand; then you can start the next row using both of the new size needles.

Row 1: (Knit 1, purl 1) across: you'll have 18 knit stitches and 18 purl stitches.

Repeat Row 1 until Lower Cuff measures 3" (7.5 cm).

Bind off all stitches loosely in **ribbing**.

You learned how to bind off knit stitches when making the Knit Coaster (page 14) and how to bind off purl stitches when making the Purl Coaster (page 19). Since ribbing is made by alternating knit stitches with purl stitches, you should bind off in the same way — knit stitches are bound off in knit and purl stitches are bound off in purl.

FINISHING

Fold the Leg Warmer lengthwise, with the **right** side facing you and the edges lined up. Weave the back seam *(see Fig. 17, page 30)*. Weave in the yarn ends.

project ideas:

Stripes are cool. Try your hand at combining scrap yarn colors for a pair of really funky Leg Warmers. Or make extra pairs to match your favorite winter outfits.

Hand Mitts

A neat alternative to gloves, these Hand Mitts are just the thing to keep your hands warm and your fingers free! Made with knit 2, purl 2 ribbing (page 21) at each end and Stockinette Stitch (page 21) between, these fun Mitts can be made in a flash!

 BEGINNER

Finished Size: 6½" around by 6" long (16.5 cm by 5 cm)

SHOPPING LIST

Yarn (Medium Weight) ![MEDIUM 4]

[6 ounces, 315 yards

(170 grams, 288 meters) per skein]:

☐ 1 skein

Knitting Needles

Straight,

☐ Size 8 (5 mm)

or size needed for gauge

(see Gauge, page 59)

Additional Supplies

☐ Yarn needle

GAUGE INFORMATION

In Stockinette Stitch *(see page 21)*,

18 stitches and 24 rows = 4" (10 cm)

Gauge Swatch: 4" (10 cm) square

Cast on 18 stitches.

Row 1 (Right side**):** Knit each stitch across the row.

Row 2: Purl each stitch across the row.

Rows 3-24: Repeat Rows 1 and 2, 11 times.

Bind off all stitches in **knit.**

MITT (Make 2)
WRIST RIBBING

Leaving a long end for sewing, cast on 32 stitches **loosely.**

Row 1: (Knit 2, purl 2) across.

Repeat Row 1 until the ribbing measures 2" (5 cm).

BODY

Work in Stockinette Stitch (knit one row, purl one row) until the piece measures 4" (10 cm) from the cast on edge, ending by working a **purl** row.

project ideas:

Go wild and seam the Mitts with the "bumpy" purl side as your right side! Or for an awesome trio, color coordinate your Mitts with the Hat and the Scarf!

PALM RIBBING

Row 1: (Knit 2, purl 2) across.

Repeat Row 1 until the ribbing measures 2" (5 cm).

Bind off all stitches in ribbing *(see page 50)*, leaving a long end for sewing.

FINISHING

Thread the yarn needle with the first long end. Fold the Mitt with the **right** side facing you and the edges lined up. Weave the Wrist Ribbing and the side of the Body for the first 2½" (6.5 cm) *(see Fig. 17, page 30)*. Weave in the yarn end.

Thread the yarn needle with the second yarn end. Weave the Palm Ribbing and the side of Body for the last 2¼" (5.5 cm), leaving a 1¼" (3 cm) opening for your thumb. Weave in the yarn end.

Hat

To make this striped Hat, you'll have to know the knit two together decrease (pages 24 & 25) and how to change colors (page 38). The new skill for this project is carrying your yarn along the *edge* of the Hat after a color change.

 **BEGINNER**

Finished Size: Fits 20" (51 cm) head circumference

SHOPPING LIST

Yarn (Medium Weight) 4

[6 ounces, 315 yards
(170 grams, 288 meters) per skein]:
☐ Blue - 1 skein
[4 ounces, 204 yards
(113 grams, 186 meters) per skein]:
☐ Variegated - 1 skein

Knitting Needles

Straight,
☐ Size 6 (4 mm) **and**
☐ Size 8 (5 mm)
  or sizes needed for gauge
  (see Gauge, page 59)

Additional Supplies

☐ Yarn needle

GAUGE INFORMATION

In Stockinette Stitch *(see page 21)*,
  18 stitches and 24 rows = 4" (10 cm)
Gauge Swatch: 4" (10 cm) square
With larger size needles, cast on
18 stitches.
Row 1 (Right side)**:** Knit each stitch
across the row.
Row 2: Purl each stitch across the
row.
Rows 3-24: Repeat Rows 1 and 2,
11 times.
Bind off all stitches in **knit**.

HAT
RIBBING

With Blue and using smaller size
needles, cast on 80 stitches **loosely**.

Rows 1-23: (Knit 2, purl 2) across:
you'll have 40 knit stitches and
40 purl stitches.

Drop Blue (do **not** cut yarn).

BODY

Begin using larger size needles
(see page 50) and change to
Variegated *(see Fig. 20, page 38)*.

Row 1: With Variegated, purl each
stitch across the row: you should
have 80 stitches total and should
continue to have 80 stitches through
Row 19.

Loosely carry each yarn not
being used along the edge of the Hat
(see Fig. 27). When you reach the end
of the row where the carried yarn is,
twist the yarn being used around the
carried strand to prevent big loops
along the edge. Don't twist too tight
because that would cause the edge
to draw up or pucker.

Fig. 27

Row 2 (Right side)**:** Knit each stitch across the row.

Rows 3 and 4: Repeat Rows 1 and 2.

Row 5: With Blue, purl each stitch across the row.

Row 6: Knit each stitch across the row.

Rows 7 and 8: Repeat Rows 5 and 6.

Rows 9-19: Repeat Rows 1-8 once, then repeat Rows 1-3 once **more**.

TOP SHAPING

Row 1: Knit 4, knit 2 stitches together *(see Figs. 12a & b, pages 24 & 25)*, (knit 8, knit 2 stitches together) across to the last 4 stitches, knit 4: you'll now have 72 stitches.

Row 2: With Blue, purl each stitch across the row.

Row 3: Knit 3, knit 2 stitches together, (knit 7, knit 2 stitches together) across to the last 4 stitches, knit 4: you'll now have 64 stitches.

Row 4: Purl each stitch across the row.

Row 5: Knit 3, knit 2 stitches together, (knit 6, knit 2 stitches together) across to the last 3 stitches, knit 3: you'll now have 56 stitches.

Row 6: With Variegated, purl each stitch across the row.

Row 7: Knit 2, knit 2 together, (knit 5, knit 2 together) across to last 3 stitches, knit 3: you'll now have 48 stitches.

Row 8: Purl each stitch across the row.

Row 9: Knit 2, knit 2 stitches together, (knit 4, knit 2 stitches together) across to the last 2 stitches, knit 2: you'll now have 40 stitches.

Row 10: With Blue, purl each stitch across the row.

Row 11: Knit 1, knit 2 stitches together, (knit 3, knit 2 stitches together) across to the last 2 stitches, knit 2: you'll now have 32 stitches.

Row 12: Purl each stitch across the row.

Row 13: Knit 1, knit 2 stitches together, (knit 2, knit 2 stitches together) across to last stitch, knit the last stitch: you'll now have 24 stitches.

Cut Blue, leaving a length that is twice as long as the Hat's edge to be used for sewing the seam.

Row 14: With Variegated, purl each stitch across the row.

Row 15: (Knit 1, knit 2 stitches together) across: you'll now have 16 stitches.

Row 16: Purl each stitch across the row.

Row 17: (Knit 2 stitches together) across: you will now have 8 stitches.

Cut Variegated, leaving a length of yarn that is twice as long as the Hat's edge to be used for sewing the seam.

Thread the yarn needle with the Variegated end and weave through the 8 stitches on the needle *(see Fig. 14, page 27)*, removing the knitting needle and pulling the stitches tightly closed. Do **not** remove yarn needle and do **not** cut yarn end.

With the **right** side of the Hat inside and lining up the rows, weave the seam *(see Fig. 17, page 30)*, using a matching yarn end and carrying each unused yarn **loosely** on the **wrong** side.

project ideas:
Make one of your stripe colors on your Hat the same as your Scarf color for a matching set.

general instructions

Knit instructions are written using abbreviations, symbols, terms and punctuation marks.

Since this is a beginner's book, there are very few abbreviations used. Here is a list of some common abbreviations used in knit books.

ABBREVIATIONS

CC	Contrasting Color
cm	centimeters
K	knit
M1	Make One
MC	Main Color
mm	millimeters
P	purl
PSSO	pass slipped stitch(es) over
Rnd(s)	Round(s)
st(s)	stitch(es)
tbl	through the back loop(s)
tog	together
YO	yarn over

TERMINOLOGY

U.S. and International terminologies are a little bit different:

KNIT TERMINOLOGY	
UNITED STATES	INTERNATIONAL
gauge =	tension
bind off =	cast off
yarn over (YO) =	yarn forward (yfwd) **or** yarn around needle (yrn)

SYMBOLS & TERMS

★ — work all instructions following a ★ (star) as many **more** times as indicated in addition to the first time.

change to larger/smaller size needles — replace the right needle with size needle specified and work the stitches from the left needle as instructed; at the end of the row, replace the left needle with the other size needle.

loosely — (casting on, adding new, or binding off stitches) the work should be as stretchy as the knitting.

right side vs. wrong side — the right side of your work is the side that will show when the piece is finished.

work even — work without increasing or decreasing in the established pattern.

PUNCTUATION

When reading knitting instructions, read from punctuation mark to punctuation mark. Just as in reading, commas (,) and semicolons (;) mean a pause.

colon (:) — the number(s) given after a colon at the end of a row tells the number of stitches you should have on that row. When repeating rows, the number given is for the last row.

parentheses ( ) or brackets [ ] — indicate a repetition, so you should work the instructions within the ( ) or [ ] as many times as it says. Information given in parentheses or brackets may also explain more about the pattern.

WHAT IS GAUGE?

Gauge is the number of stitches and rows per inch or centimeters and is used to determine the finished size of a project. Most knitting patterns specify the gauge that you must match to make sure your project fits right and that you'll have enough yarn to complete your project.

Before beginning a pattern that gives a gauge, it's absolutely necessary for you to knit a sample swatch in the pattern stitch with the weight of yarn and needle size suggested. The swatch must be large enough for you to measure your gauge, usually a 4" (10 cm) square. After completing the swatch, measure it. If your swatch is larger or smaller than specified, make another, changing needle size to get the correct gauge.

Remember, DO NOT HESITATE TO CHANGE NEEDLE SIZE IN ORDER TO OBTAIN CORRECT GAUGE. Once you have obtained correct gauge, you should continue to measure the total width of your work every 3-4" (7.5-10 cm) to be sure your gauge does not change.

For many of the projects in this book, gauge doesn't really matter that much. The Posy and the Coasters can certainly be a little bigger or smaller without changing the overall effect. However, most knit patterns specify the gauge that you must match.

Yarn Weight Symbol & Names	LACE 0	SUPER FINE 1	FINE 2	LIGHT 3	MEDIUM 4	BULKY 5	SUPER BULKY 6	JUMBO 7
Type of Yarns in Category	Fingering, size 10 crochet thread	Sock, Fingering, Baby	Sport, Baby	DK, Light Worsted	Worsted, Afghan, Aran	Chunky, Craft, Rug	Super Bulky, Roving	Jumbo, Roving
Knit Gauge Ranges in Stockinette St to 4" (10 cm)	33-40 sts**	27-32 sts	23-26 sts	21-24 sts	16-20 sts	12-15 sts	7-11 sts	6 sts and fewer
Advised Needle Size Range	000 to 1	1 to 3	3 to 5	5 to 7	7 to 9	9 to11	11 to 17	17 and larger

* GUIDELINES ONLY: The chart above reflects the most commonly used gauges and needle sizes for specific yarn categories.

** Lace weight yarns are usually knitted on larger needles to create lacy openwork patterns. Accordingly, a gauge range is difficult to determine. Always follow the gauge stated in your pattern.

KNITTING NEEDLES																			
U.S.	0	1	2	3	4	5	6	7	8	9	10	10½	11	13	15	17	19	35	50
U.K.	13	12	11	10	9	8	7	6	5	4	3	2	1	00	000	---	---	---	---
Metric - mm	2	2.25	2.75	3.25	3.5	3.75	4	4.5	5	5.5	6	6.5	8	9	10	12.75	15	19	25

SKILL LEVELS

An icon that looks like the one above can be found at the top of a pattern and lets you know the skill level that the pattern requires.

Every pattern in this book is ranked by the icon that you find at the top of page under the title. The chart at the right explains the skill level icons and how they are used.

⬛⬜⬜⬜ BEGINNER	Projects for first-time knitters using basic knit and purl stitches. Minimal shaping.
⬛⬛⬜⬜ EASY	Projects using basic stitches, repetitive stitch patterns, simple color changes, and simple shaping and finishing.
⬛⬛⬛⬜ INTERMEDIATE	Projects with a variety of stitches, such as basic cables and lace, simple intarsia, double-pointed needles and knitting in the round needle techniques, mid-level shaping and finishing.
⬛⬛⬛⬛ EXPERIENCED	Projects using advanced techniques and stitches, such as short rows, fair isle, more intricate intarsia, cables, lace patterns, and numerous color changes.

DROPPED STITCHES

A dropped stitch is a stitch that accidentally slips off the needle and can easily unravel for more than one row. 📹 To fix a dropped stitch, hold the work with the knit side facing in Stockinette Stitch **or** with a purl stitch below the last loop in Garter Stitch or Seed Stitch *(see Fig. 28a)*. Insert a crochet hook through the loop of the dropped stitch, hook the strand of yarn immediately above it *(see Fig. 28b)*, and pull it through the loop on your hook. Continue in this manner until you have used all of the strands of yarn, turning the work after every strand when working in Garter Stitch or Seed Stitch **only**. Slip the stitch onto the left needle with the right side of the stitch to the **front** *(see Fig. 29)*.

Fig. 28a

Fig. 28b

FRONT AND BACK LOOPS

Always work into the front loop of a stitch unless instructed to work through back loop *(see Fig. 29)*.

Fig. 29

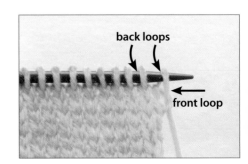

back loops

front loop

SLIPPING STITCHES

Slipping stitches means that you will be moving a stitch from the left needle to the right needle **without** working into it. When slipping stitches, 🎥 slip the stitch as if to **purl** if you're not going to use the slipped stitch again until the next row *(see Fig. 30a)*. Keep the front loop to the front. If you're going to use the slipped stitch again on the same row, as in a decrease, 🎥 slip it as if to **knit** *(see Fig. 30b)*.

Fig. 30a

Fig. 30b

YARN OVERS

To make a yarn over, you'll loop the yarn over the needle like you would to knit or purl a stitch, bringing it either to the front or the back of the piece so that it'll be ready to work the next stitch, creating a new stitch on the needle and a lacy hole in the fabric.

🎥 **Between two knit stitches**

Bring the yarn forward **between** the needles, then back **over** the top of the right needle, so that it's now in position to knit the next stitch *(see Fig. 31a)*.

Fig. 31a

🎥 Between two purl stitches

Take the yarn **over** the right needle to the back, then forward **under** it, so that it's now in position to purl the next stitch *(see Fig. 31b)*.

Fig. 31b

🎥 After a knit stitch, before a purl stitch

Take the yarn forward **between** the needles, then back **over** the top of the right needle and forward **between** the needles again, so that it's now in position to purl the next stitch *(see Fig. 31c)*.

Fig. 31c

🎥 After a purl stitch, before a knit stitch

Take the yarn **over** the right needle to the back, so that it's now in position to knit the next stitch *(see Fig. 31d)*.

Fig. 31d

CHANGING COLORS

Always start a new ball or skein at the beginning or end of a row, never in the middle *(see Fig. 32a)*. The yarn can be carried up the side, twisting it every few rows *(see Fig. 32b)* or it can be cut, leaving an end at least as long as your hand. The ends can be woven into the edge or in the back of the work.

Fig. 32a

Fig. 32b

yarn information

Each item in this book was made using Medium Weight Yarn. Any brand of Medium Weight Yarn may be used. It's best to refer to the yardage/meters when determining how many balls or skeins to purchase. Remember, to arrive at the finished size, it is the GAUGE/TENSION that is most important, not the brand of yarn.

For your convenience, listed below are the specific yarns used to create our photography models. Because yarn manufacturers make frequent changes in their product lines, you may sometimes find it necessary to use a substitute yarn or to search for the discontinued product at alternate suppliers (locally or online).

KNIT COASTER
Lion Brand® Kitchen Cotton
#147 Grape

PURL COASTER
Lily® Sugar'n Cream®
#02741 Playtime Ombre

OPEN PETAL POSY
Caron® Simply Soft®
#9782 Gold
#9610 Grape
#9604 Watermelon
#9608 Blue Mint
#9777 Neon Green
Caron® Simply Soft® Paints
#0016 Rainbow Bright

COTTON WASHCLOTH
Lily® Sugar'n Cream®
#00010 Yellow

SOFT DRINK COZY
Lily® Sugar'n Cream®
#02741 Playtime Ombre

DOG'S TOY BALL
Caron® Simply Soft®
Small Ball - #9782 Gold
Medium Ball - #9774 Neon Orange
Large Ball - #9782 Gold
   #9774 Neon Orange
   #9777 Neon Green

SCARF
Caron® Simply Soft®
#9608 Blue Mint

RIPPLE LAP WRAP
Caron® Simply Soft®
Purple - #9610 Grape
Pink - #9604 Watermelon
Blue - #9608 Blue Mint
Green - #9777 Neon Green
Yellow - #9782 Gold
Caron® Simply Soft® Paints
Variegated - #0016 Rainbow Bright

PILLOW
Caron® Simply Soft®
Blue - #9608 Blue Mint
Yellow - #9782 Gold
Purple - #9610 Grape
Green - #9777 Neon Green

CAT'S TOY FISH
Caron® Simply Soft®
#9608 Blue Mint
#9782 Gold
#9774 Neon Orange

LEG WARMERS
Caron® Simply Soft®
#9610 Grape

HAND MITTS
Caron® Simply Soft®
#9608 Blue Mint

HAT
Caron® Simply Soft®
Blue - #9608 Blue Mint
Caron® Simply Soft® Paints
Variegated - #0011 Peacock Feather

We have made every effort to ensure that these instructions are accurate and complete. We cannot, however, be responsible for human error, typographical mistakes, or variations in individual work.

Production Team: Instructional/Technical Editor - Sarah J. Green; Editorial Writer - Susan Frantz Wiles; Senior Graphic Artist - Lora Puls; Photo Stylist - Lori Wenger; and Photographers - Jason Masters and Ken West.

Items made and instructions tested by Raymelle Greening.

Library of Congress Control Number: 2015954900